PowerKiDS Readers

MY COMMUNITY

A TRIP TO THE
HOSPITAL

Josie Keogh

PowerKiDS press.

New York

Published in 2013 by The Rosen Publishing Group, Inc.
29 East 21st Street, New York, NY 10010

First Edition

Editor: Amelie von Zumbusch
Book Design: Ashley Drago

Photo Credits: Cover © www.iStockphoto.com/Nicole Waring; p. 5 Sozaijiten/Datacraft/Getty Images; p. 6 Alexander Raths/Shutterstock.com; p. 9 Comstock/Thinkstock; pp. 10, 13 Monkey Business Images/Shutterstock.com; p. 14 Fotokostic/Shutterstock.com; p. 17 Minerva Studio/Shutterstock.com; p. 18 ERproductions Ltd/Blend Images/Getty Images; p. 21 © www.iStockphoto.com/Rich Legg; p. 22 Donald Joski/Shutterstock.com; p. 24 Stephen Coburn/Shutterstock.com.

Library of Congress Cataloging-in-Publication Data

Keogh, Josie.
  A trip to the hospital / by Josie Keogh. — 1st ed.
    p. cm. — (Powerkids readers: my community)
  Includes index.
  ISBN 978-1-4488-7407-1 (library binding) — ISBN 978-1-4488-7486-6 (pbk.) —
ISBN 978-1-4488-7560-3 (6-pack)
  1. Hospitals—Juvenile literature. 2. Children—Hospital care–Juvenile literature. I. Title.
  RA963.5.K46 2013
  362.11—dc23
                                    2011052017

Manufactured in the United States of America

CPSIA Compliance Information: Batch #CS12PK: For Further Information contact Rosen Publishing, New York, New York at 1-800-237-9932

CONTENTS

June went to the hospital.

Her dad is sick.

7

Pete visits his grandpa.

Kit sleeps there.

She has been there for a month.

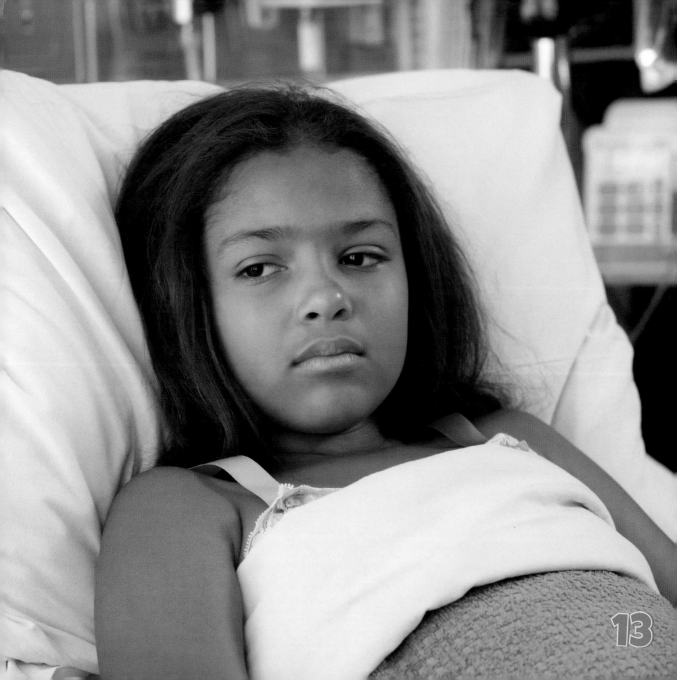

14

Ed hurt his foot.

Dr. Hay met with Ed.

She gave him a cast.

Luke met his new sister.

21

She is one day old.

WORDS TO KNOW

doctor: A person who treats sick people.

nurse: A person who cares for sick people.

patient: A person who is sick.

INDEX

WEBSITES

Due to the changing nature of Internet links, PowerKids Press has developed an online list of websites related to the subject of this book. This site is updated regularly. Please use this link to access the list: www.powerkidslinks.com/pkrc/hosp/